THE STORY OF Aircraft

THE FIRST AIRCRAFT to lift people off Earth's surface was a hot-air balloon built by brothers Joseph and Etienne Montgolfier, who discovered that an air-filled paper bag would rise. They made a model linen balloon, added a wicker basket, and sent a sheep, a cockerel and a duck on a short flight before the astonished gaze of King Louis XVI. Later that year, on 21 November, Pilâtre de Rozier and the Marquis d'Arlandes became the first aviators in history when their paper-lined linen balloon (left) lifted off to a height of 85 metres. Powered by the rising hot air from a fire of burning straw, *Montgolfière* drifted over Paris for 25 minutes before landing 8.5 kilometres away.

Later balloons used hydrogen instead of hot air, but all types lacked any means of steering. Changing the gas-bag to a cigar-shape design, fitting a RUDDER and adding an engine provided the answer – and so the airship was born. From the early 1900s rigid airships were built with a metal skeleton, and a fabric outer cover. Giant gas cells, each separated by fabric walls, occupied the space inside.

Some of the first rigid airships were designed by the German Count von Zeppelin. Soon, they served both as luxury airliners – and fearsome weapons of war. During the First World War, Zeppelins carried out bombing raids on London. Airships achieved their greatest glory in the 1920s and 30s. The size of ocean liners, huge craft like the *Graf Zeppelin* toured the world with passengers enjoying luxurious accommodation inside the hull.

▶ SHORT S.27 TANDEM TWIN (1911)

Now that people had learnt to fly aeroplanes, the search was on for more power. The Gnome ROTARY ENGINE appeared in 1909 and quickly became the standard design for most aircraft. On the Tandem Twin, the pilot sat between two engines, so it became known as the 'Gnome Sandwich'. It was a much safer plane as it could still fly on only one engine.

▼ WRIGHT BROTHERS' FLYER 1 (1903)

Orville and Wilbur Wright will always be remembered for their historic achievement: the first controlled, powered flight by an aeroplane. The American brothers gained their success by learning first how to fly, then building a machine that they could control. *Flyer 1* was based on gliders they had designed earlier, incorporating a mechanism which enabled the pilot to twist or 'warp' the wings, and thus roll the aircraft to the left or right. On the sand dunes of Kitty Hawk, North Carolina, with Orville at the controls, *Flyer 1* flew for 12 seconds before grounding 36.6 metres away. The date was 17 December 1903.

▲ VOISIN-FARMAN I (1907)

Henry Farman, an Englishman living in Paris, was the first European to fly a practical, controllable aeroplane. After teaching himself how to fly it, he was the first person to make a flight taking off and landing at the same place. His 1908 trip across northern France was the world's first long-distance flight.

▲ BLÉRIOT XI (1909)

Frenchman Louis Blériot was the first to cross the English Channel by air. The flight won him a £1000 prize offered by the London *Daily Mail*. With no means of navigation (he simply asked a bystander 'Which way is England?'), he set off into the mist and crash-landed above the cliffs of Dover 37 minutes later. Blériot became an instant celebrity and sold more than 100 of his MONOPLANES. Meanwhile, people began to realise what a formidable weapon of war the aeroplane might be.

PIONEERS

All aircraft drawn to scale

AT THE CONTROLS

IN THE DRIVING SEAT
Seated on the flight deck are the pilot (the Captain, on the left) and co-pilot (the First Officer, on the right), with room for extra crew members to sit behind them. Behind the COCKPIT there are rest bunks, where the pilots can take a break (not at the same time!) on a long, tiring flight. Now that advanced digital technology can give the pilots regular updates on the aircraft's mechanical condition throughout the flight, there is no need for a third member of the crew, the Flight Engineer, in the cockpit of a modern Boeing 747-400.

For much of any journey, the controls are switched to an automatic control system, or AUTOPILOT. It uses computers to sense outside conditions, such as wind speed, and to manipulate the controls accordingly to travel along a pre-set route. All the crew have to do is to keep an eye on the monitors to check that all systems are functioning correctly.

For safety reasons, a Boeing 747 is equipped with a cockpit voice recorder and a flight recorder, sometimes known as the 'black box' (although it is actually a bright orange colour). These instruments always record every manoeuvre the aircraft makes during a flight. In the event of an incident or, worse, a crash, the recordings can be played back and perhaps provide evidence for what went wrong.

At the Jumbo's nose is the radome, containing a powerful RADAR. Constantly transmitting and receiving back radio signals, it enables the crew to watch ahead for other aircraft and approaching storms.

FLIGHT PANEL DISPLAYS
Six cathode ray tube (CRT) displays – three for each pilot – give all the information needed to fly the plane. (If any CRT display goes wrong, the pilots can switch to manual displays. These are most of the other dials on the flight panel.)

The Primary Flight Display (PFD) shows the aeroplane's attitude – the angle at which it is flying in relation to the Earth. An artificial horizon on the screen represents the Earth's surface, and a fixed bar represents the plane's wings. If it banks (makes a rolling turn) to the left or right, the bar will be displayed at an angle to the horizon. The PFD also indicates the plane's course, its speed – both the rate at which it is climbing or descending and its speed through the air – and the height of the plane above the land or sea it is flying over. It gives the pilot the information he needs to perform a 'blind' landing (landing the aircraft in dense fog).

The Navigation Display (ND) shows a map of the route, plotting the plane's position, and featuring all the navigation points on the ground. It gives estimated arrival times at waypoints (pre-set positions strung out along the route) and indications of wind directions and speeds.

The Engine Indication and Crew Alerting System (EICAS) gives extensive up-to-the-second information about the operation of the aeroplane's systems and engines. The crew can check at any time that all four engines are functioning correctly.

KEY TO FLIGHT PANEL
58 OVERHEAD SWITCH PANELS (to turn systems on or off)
59 SYSTEMS CONTROLS (hydraulics, de-icing, air conditioning, electricity, etc.)
60 INTEGRATED FLIGHT CONTROL (IFC) PANEL (for autopilot)
61 FAULT CAUTION
62 SELECTOR SWITCHES (for panels and instruments)
63 PFD
64 ND
65 EICAS
66 CLOCK
67 STANDBY DISPLAYS
68 THROTTLES
69 FLIGHT MANAGEMENT COMPUTER SYSTEM
70 FLAP LEVER
71 COMMUNICATIONS RADIO
72 YOKE OR WHEEL (for manual flying)
73 PASSENGER-CABIN INSTRUCTIONS CONTROL

CABIN COMFORTS

Normally, the Jumbo carries 420 passengers, 21 in First Class, 77 in Business Class and 322 in Economy Class, but the seating can be re-arranged to accommodate many more. (A special type of the 747-400 flown in Japan is designed to carry 569 passengers.) Galleys and lavatories can also be re-positioned to allow extra seating to be put in.

Passengers stow their 'carry-on' luggage (items they have brought on to the aircraft with them) in overhead luggage compartments. For each person there are fold-away tables, reading lamps, air vents, and headsets that can be plugged into music programmes, or the soundtrack to a film shown on a small cinema screen. Passengers' seats can be adjusted to lean backwards. During the journey, flight attendants serve food and drinks from trolleys wheeled up and down the aisles.

KEY

- 45 EMERGENCY DOOR
- 46 LAVATORY
- 47 ANTI-COLLISION LIGHT
- 48 FORWARD BAGGAGE HOLD
- 49 UPPER DECK SEATING
- 50 PILOTS' REST BUNKS
- 51 COCKPIT OR FLIGHT DECK
- 52 RUDDER PEDALS
- 53 FIRST-CLASS SEATING
- 54 WHEEL RETRACTION HYDRAULICS
- 55 STEERING MECHANISM
- 56 NOSE GEAR
- 57 RADOME

The nose LANDING GEAR *has two wheels positioned side by side. On take-off, they retract in a forward direction into the nose of the* FUSELAGE, *powered by* HYDRAULIC *jacks. Hinged doors close behind them.*

THE WORLD'S LARGEST AIRLINER

- The Boeing 747 can travel a third of the way round the world – more than 13,000 kilometres – without refuelling. 747s regularly fly non-stop between New York and Seoul, London and Singapore, Buenos Aires and Frankfurt, and other distant cities.

- Boeing 747s the world over have, between them, flown about 30 billion kilometres since the plane was first launched. That is more than two hundred times the distance from Earth to the Sun.

- When parked on the runway, the tail height of the 747 is 19.41 metres, as high as a six-storey building. The TAILPLANE span is 22.17 metres, greater than the main wingspan on some airliners!

- The world's first powered flight by an aeroplane, the Wright brothers' *Flyer 1*, travelled just 37 metres at Kitty Hawk in December 1903. That is eight metres *shorter* than the length of the Economy-Class section of the 747-400. Two such flights would have taken *Flyer 1* only just past the entire length of the Jumbo (71 metres).

- Five and a half tonnes of food supplies are needed on a long-haul international flight.

- More than 160 kilometres of electrical wiring run through the aircraft. The total electricity used could provide all the energy requirements of a small town.

▶ **SPAD S.XIII (1917)**
Quick in the air and equipped with twin machine guns, the French-designed Spad S.XIII BIPLANE was one of the most successful fighters of the First World War on the Allies' side. It proved an equal match for the German Fokkers.

▶ **FOKKER Dr.I (1917)**
During the First World War, Anthony Fokker, a Dutch designer who was working for the Germans, invented an interrupter gear for the aircraft engine. This device allowed a machine gun to fire forward without hitting the aeroplane's own propeller. Fokker aircraft proceeded to dominate the skies, a time the Allies called the 'Fokker Scourge'. Fokker later built a TRIPLANE, copying a British model that could climb superbly and offer a better field of vision. The Dr.I was the favourite plane of famous war ace Manfred von Richthofen. He led a group of pilots known as the 'Flying Circus' into devastating, swarming attacks on enemy aircraft. Circus planes were painted bright colours, like the shields of medieval knights. Von Richthofen's was scarlet, hence his nickname, the 'Red Baron'.

■ **USS AKRON (1931)**
The *Akron* airship was built for the United States Navy as a scouting craft, reporting back on the enemy's naval positions. Measuring 239 metres in length (longer than two football pitches placed end to end), she had eight engines that could drive her forward at nearly 130 km/h. Her life was short, however. On the night of 3 April 1933, a storm forced her to crash into the sea: all but three of the 76 people on board perished.

▼ **FARMAN GOLIATH (1919)**
Soon after the end of the war, aircraft designers were busy converting bombers into airliners. A Farman Goliath, fitted out with two cabins, made the first passenger flight from Paris to London, with 11 people on board. Soon, it opened the first regular scheduled international passenger service with weekly flights from Paris to Brussels.

▲ **SIKORSKY *LE GRAND* (1913)**
The world's largest aeroplane in its day, *Bolshoi Baltiskii* (Great Baltic) or *Le Grand* was also the first to be equipped with four engines. For its time, it was huge: its wingspan (28 metres) almost the same as a DC-3 of 20 years later. Russian engineer Igor Sikorsky designed an improved version of it the following year. Called the *Ilya Mourometz*, it was fitted with a heated lounge for passengers, and a promenade deck above the FUSELAGE. Here brave souls could take a stroll more than 1000 metres up with little more than a light rail to hold on to! *Le Grand* and the *Ilya Mourometz* were the forerunners of the long-range bombers and airliners.

■ *Inside her hull, the Akron carried a 'spy basket', an observation car dangling at the end of a long steel cable uncoiled from the mother ship. It was a human periscope: an observer sitting in the car would report on enemy positions by telephone up to the airship hidden above the clouds.*

▼ JUNKERS Ju 87 STUKA (1935)

Called the Stuka after the German word for dive-bomber, this aircraft was one of the most feared weapons of the Second World War. As well as the bombs it carried, it was armed with machine guns. The high-pitched whine that screamed through the air as it dived struck terror into all who heard it.

▼ CONSOLIDATED B-24 LIBERATOR (1940)

By the time the Second World War had broken out, large planes capable of flying more than 3000 kilometres without refuelling were being built. Attacks from the air by bombers such as the American B-24 could now be launched from great distances.

▼ MITSUBISHI A6M ZERO (1940)

In December 1941 Japanese forces attacked the US fleet stationed at Pearl Harbor, Hawaii. Their fighter planes ruled the Pacific skies during the early years of the war. The Zero was the best of them. Taking off from aircraft carriers, these lightly-built aircraft climbed rapidly and manoeuvred well in the skies.

▼ LOCKHEED CONSTELLATION (1943)

By the end of the Second World War there were a great many large, high-capacity, long-range aeroplanes about, and plenty of good airfields with long runways for them to fly between. After the war, airlines in the United States and Europe were quick to cater for the many people who were now quite accustomed to flying to all parts of the world. Bombers and transporters were converted to airliners, among them the Constellation. Seating up to 65 passengers in a PRESSURIZED CABIN and speeding them to their destination at around 500 km/h, this American aeroplane was deservedly crowned 'Queen of the Skies'. Later models, called Super Constellations, had extra fuel tanks in pods on their wingtips enabling them to fly non-stop across the Atlantic.

▶ MESSERSCHMITT Me 262 (1944)

German aircraft were the first to take to the skies fitted with TURBOJET engines. The Me 262 fighter-bomber, together with the British Gloster Meteor, were the first jets to see action in the Second World War. The 262's powerful jet engines powered it to speeds of 800 km/h, more than 150 km/h faster than the Allies' fastest fighter. The jet age had truly begun.

◀ SUPERMARINE SPITFIRE (1936)

Striving for supremacy in the air during the Second World War, aircraft manufacturers constantly worked on improvements to their top fighters to make them more powerful and better-armed. Many different versions of the German Messerschmitt Bf 109 and Focke-Wulf Fw 190 appeared throughout the war. Nearly 23,000 Spitfires, in 40 different models, were built between 1936 and 1947, more than any other British aircraft. Quick and nimble, with a powerful Rolls-Royce engine, it is famous for the part it played, along with the Hawker Hurricane, in combating German fighters and bombers during the Battle of Britain in 1940.

▲ SIKORSKY R-4 (1942)

The first helicopters appeared in the late 1930s, once engineers had worked out how to stop the aircraft twisting out of control. Igor Sikorsky's design for a helicopter with a tail ROTOR set at right angles to the main ROTOR was favoured. The first type to go into production, the R-4 soon proved its value in tight manoeuvres.

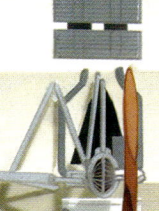

▲ ILYUSHIN Il-2 STURMOVIK (1939)

More Il-2s were built (36,000) than any other aircraft. Armed to the teeth with guns and bombs, this armour-plated Russian ground-attack aircraft proved difficult to shoot down.

■ As engine fuel was used up, Akron loaded up with water to replace the lost weight. Where did it come from? Condensers, the bands of dark patches on the hull, took in steam rising from the engine exhausts and turned it into water.

Akron's engines were carried inside the hull, while the propellers were mounted outside. The blades could turn in either direction, producing either forward or backward movement, and could be swivelled to manoeuvre the vessel up or down.

INSIDE THE BODY

The Boeing 747 is a miracle of modern engineering. It is assembled from no less than six million parts (of which about half are fasteners or rivets) made in 33 different countries.

The main body of the aeroplane, known as the FUSELAGE, is a framework of beams and ribs in the shape of a large tube. Under construction, it looks like the inside of a whale. All the parts are made of lightweight aluminium alloys (aluminium mixed with other metals like copper and zinc to make it tougher). The outer skin, also made out of aluminium alloy, is just five millimetres thick. Installed between it and the internal panels are soundproof and heat-resistant insulation materials. Only 19 centimetres of wall separate the passengers from their warm, comfortable cabin and the freezing, air-less atmosphere more than 10 kilometres above ground!

The fuselage is assembled in three main sections, each lowered into position by cranes. The centre body is fitted to the wing assembly, followed by the front and rear sections.

Up to 270 kilograms of paint are used on the plane's exterior.

HOME OF THE 747

The main assembly building for the world's largest airliner is also the largest building, by volume, in the world. Dug out of forested slopes north of Seattle, Washington state, the Everett manufacturing plant stands 11 storeys high and has a floor space equivalent to the area of 750 football pitches! Employees are equipped with bicycles to get around the factory, and a railway track runs right into the building. Enough power is used to light more than 32,000 homes. The Everett plant even has its own fire station and police force.

KEY
24 THRUST REVERSE OUTLETS
25 ENGINE COWLING
26 LANDING GEAR WHEEL BOGIE
27 WHEEL RETRACTION HYDRAULICS
28 EMERGENCY DOOR
29 COMMUNICATIONS AERIAL
30 AIR SUPPLY DUCTS
31 FUEL DISTRIBUTION PIPE
32 OVERHEAD LUGGAGE COMPARTMENTS
33 EXTERIOR OF ENGINE
34 ENGINE AIR INTAKE
35 GALLEY (KITCHEN) UNITS
36 WATER TANK
37 AIR CONDITIONING INTAKE DUCTS
38 STAIRCASE TO UPPER DECK
39 FAN
40 COMPRESSOR
41 FAN DRIVE SHAFT
42 COMBUSTION CHAMBER
43 TURBINES
44 EXHAUST GASES

POWER ON THE WINGS

Three different makes of engine can be used to power a Boeing 747-400: they are Pratt & Whitney PW4056, General Electric CF6-80C2, or (illustrated here) Rolls-Royce RB211-524G. There are four engines in all, two on each wing, contained within engine cowlings (casings) attached to the wing undersides. The front entrance to the engine, known as the intake, is so large a person could stand in it.

The Jumbo's engines are immensely powerful. Just one engine on a 747-400 produces more thrust (about 25,000 kilograms) than all four engines on a Boeing 707 put together.

ON THE GROUND

The 747-400 has 18 wheels. Two are positioned beneath the nose. The other 16, together known as the LANDING GEAR, are located beneath the centre of the plane. This many are needed to spread its enormous weight on the runway. The main landing gear consists of four four-wheeled carriages or bogies, one under each of the wings and two on the underside of the FUSELAGE. The huge impact of landing is absorbed evenly by all four bogies through their shock absorbers. Each tyre is 1.25 metres in diameter, filled with nitrogen gas and fitted with anti-skid brakes.

An air conditioning system circulates air via a network of ducts around the pressure cabin. When full of high-pressure air the aeroplane's take-off weight is increased by about a tonne.

FORWARD THRUST

The Boeing 747 is the only airliner which has an upper deck. Reached by a staircase from the lower deck, it seats 52 Business-Class passengers or 69 Economy-Class passengers. The 747-400 has, like its predecessor, the 747-300, a longer upper deck than the original version.

TURBOFAN ENGINE
The 747 engine is a type of GAS TURBINE (another name for a jet engine) called a TURBOFAN. All jets work on the same principle: air is drawn in, compressed by spinning blades, mixed with kerosene fuel and burned in a combustion chamber. The hot exhaust gas escapes at speed through the rear of the engine, turning a turbine (which drives the compressor) as it spurts past. The backward-flowing air provides a forward thrust, like the kick of a rifle after a bullet is fired.

In a turbofan, air is sucked into the engine by a whirling fan (driven by another turbine at the rear of the engine) in front of the compressor. Some of the inflowing air is ducted around the combustion chamber to join the exhaust gas. Besides being a lot more powerful than other types, the engine is cooler and quieter, and more economical in its use of fuel.

Turbofan engines are equipped with thrust reversers. When in use, the jet of hot exhaust gases is deflected forwards instead of backwards, producing a force which rapidly slows down the plane landing or the runway.

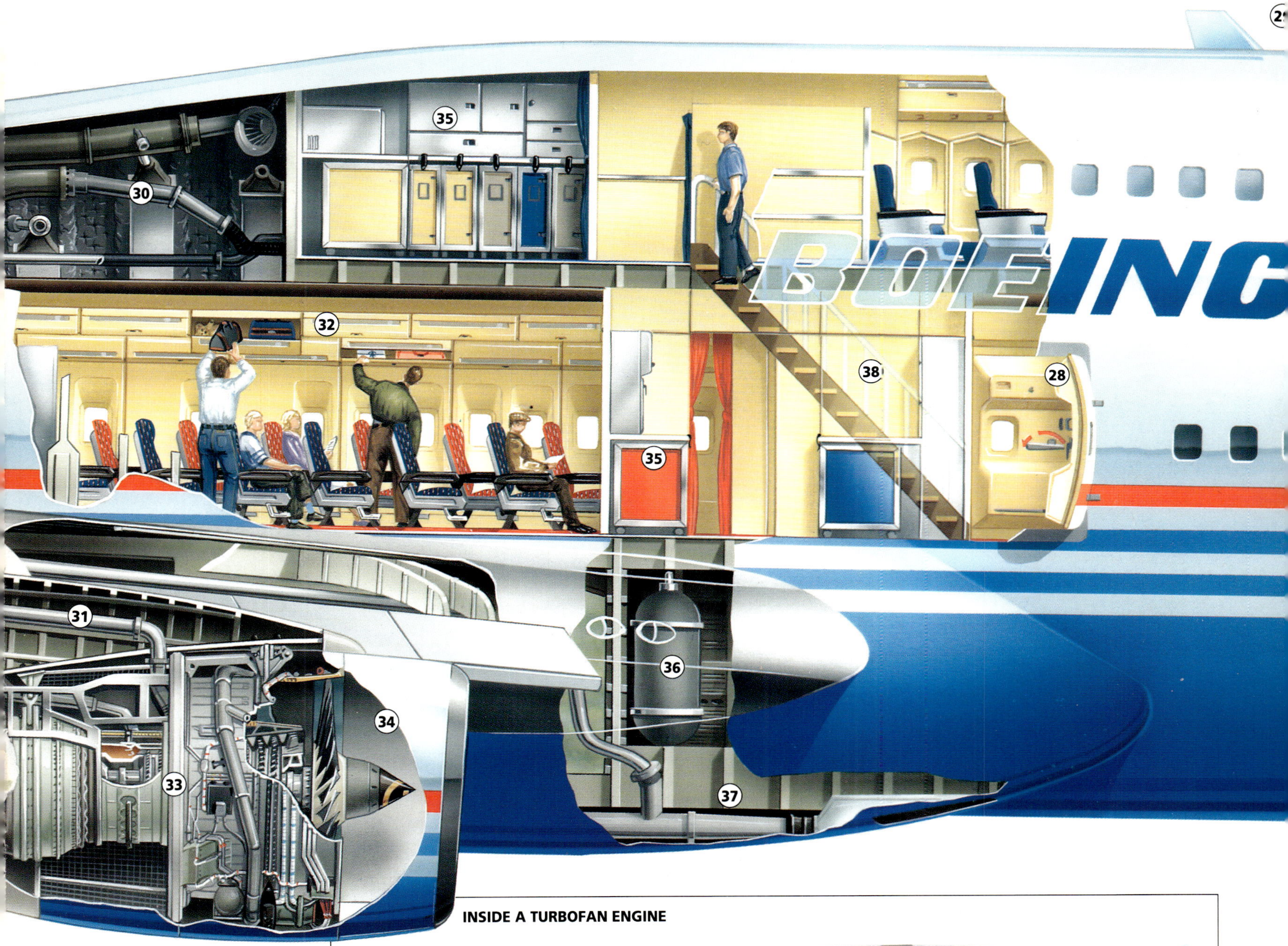

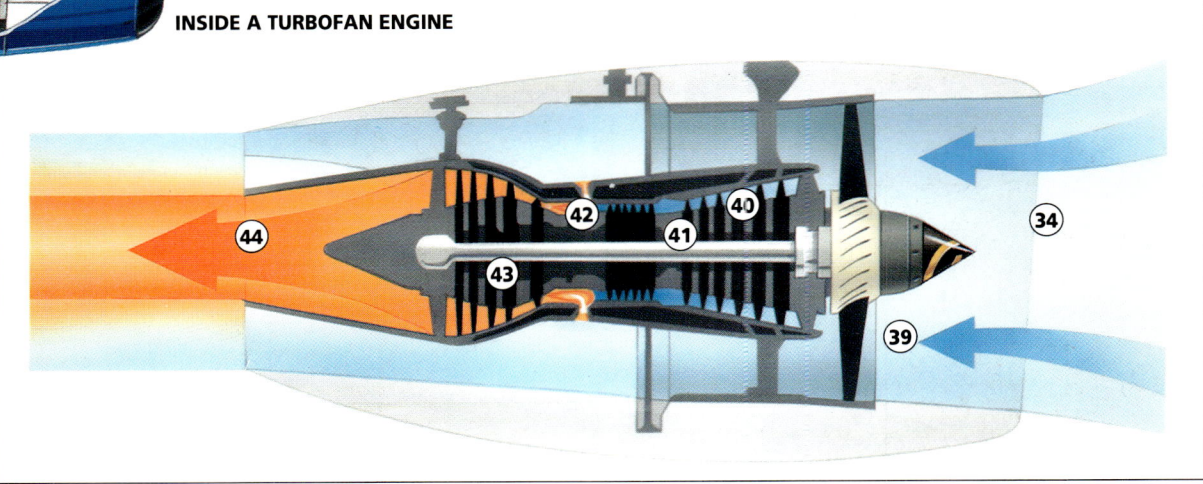

INSIDE A TURBOFAN ENGINE

ELECTRICITY AND AIR
Besides driving the plane through the air, the engines supply the power needed for the electricity used on board and to work its family of HYDRAULIC pumps. A gearbox takes power from the engine to drive, amongst other things, an electric generator. Air is also diverted from the engine compressor to pressurize the cabin.

Hot air is also used to prevent icing on the wings and at the intake section of each engine.

WINGS ACROSS THE WORLD

◀ **MARTIN B-10 (1932)**
During the First World War, and for many years afterwards, many bombers were wooden BIPLANES with open COCKPITS (like the Farman Goliath). The Martin Bomber revolutionized bomber design. Faster than most fighters of its day, this American all-metal MONOPLANE had a fully enclosed cockpit, bombs loaded in an internal bay closed by powered doors and a rotating gun turret above the nose.

▼ **DOUGLAS DC-3 DAKOTA (1935)**
Intense competition raged between rival airlines and aircraft manufacturers in the United States in the 1930s. Boeing had produced its 10-passenger Model 247 for United Airlines in 1933. The forerunner of all modern airliners, the 247 had retractable LANDING GEAR, and could cruise on only one engine. Douglas produced even better aircraft for TWA and American Airlines. Their DC-3, faster than many fighters, had a long range and a fine reputation for reliability. Hundreds are still flying today.

◀ **HANDLEY PAGE HP.42 (1930)**
Passenger air transport in the 1930s was affordable only by the very few. Britain's Imperial Airways linked the mother country with different parts of its empire in Africa and Asia. The Handley Page HP.42 was a huge, four-engined BIPLANE with its wings mounted high above its FUSELAGE. It could carry up to 38 passengers who expected, and received, luxurious service.

◀ **POLIKARPOV I-16 (1933)**
This short, stubby Soviet fighter, nicknamed the 'Little Donkey', was the first MONOPLANE fighter to have retractable wheels and a fully enclosed COCKPIT.

AKRON

◀ **SPIRIT OF ST. LOUIS (1927)**
American Charles Lindbergh was the first to fly solo across the Atlantic Ocean. It took his tiny MONOPLANE 33½ hours to complete the journey from New York to Paris. Using very simple navigation techniques, Lindbergh battled against bad weather conditions and lack of sleep to stay on course.

◀ **DORNIER DO X (1929)**
Flying Boats, which took off and landed on water, flew long-range passenger routes in the 1920s and 1930s. With a wingspan as wide as a football pitch, the Dornier Do X was the largest of these – indeed of all aeroplanes so far built. On an early flight, it took off with 169 people on board: 10 crew, 150 passengers – and 9 stowaways! Equipped with 12 engines mounted above the wing, this German aircraft was nevertheless very slow (it once took 10 *months* to cross from Germany to New York!) and strained to reach a maximum height of only 500 metres when fully loaded.

▲ **SHORT S.23 EMPIRE (1936)**
Empire flying boats – known as 'C' Class because all their names began with C – represented the height of luxury for adventurous travellers. They were intended to carry mail and up to 24 passengers on long-distance routes throughout the British Empire. Later, they were adapted to carry, piggy-back fashion, a smaller aeroplane. At a safe height, the two aircraft would separate, the aeroplane flying on to deliver the mail while the flying boat returned to base.

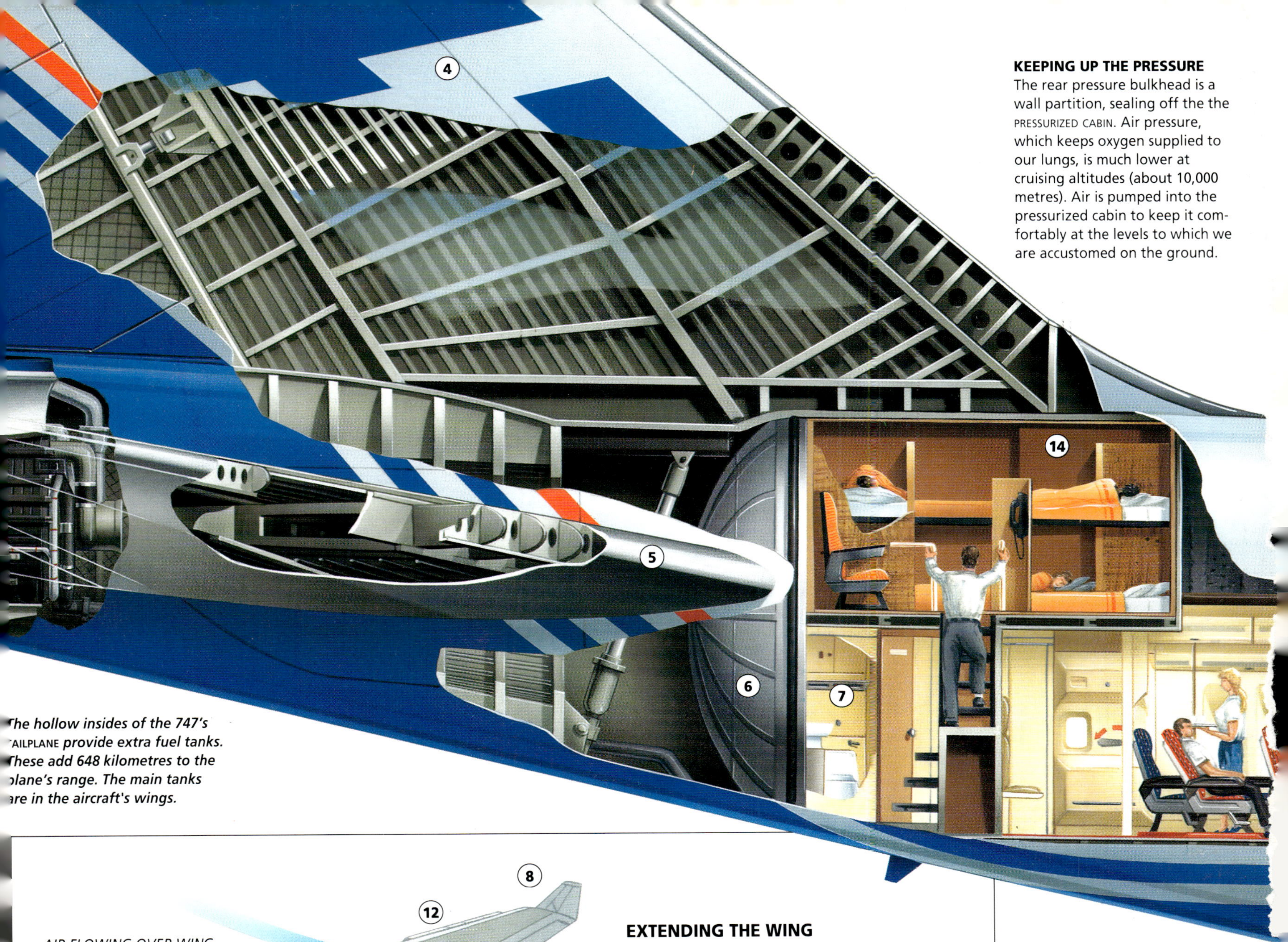

KEEPING UP THE PRESSURE
The rear pressure bulkhead is a wall partition, sealing off the the PRESSURIZED CABIN. Air pressure, which keeps oxygen supplied to our lungs, is much lower at cruising altitudes (about 10,000 metres). Air is pumped into the pressurized cabin to keep it comfortably at the levels to which we are accustomed on the ground.

The hollow insides of the 747's TAILPLANE provide extra fuel tanks. These add 648 kilometres to the plane's range. The main tanks are in the aircraft's wings.

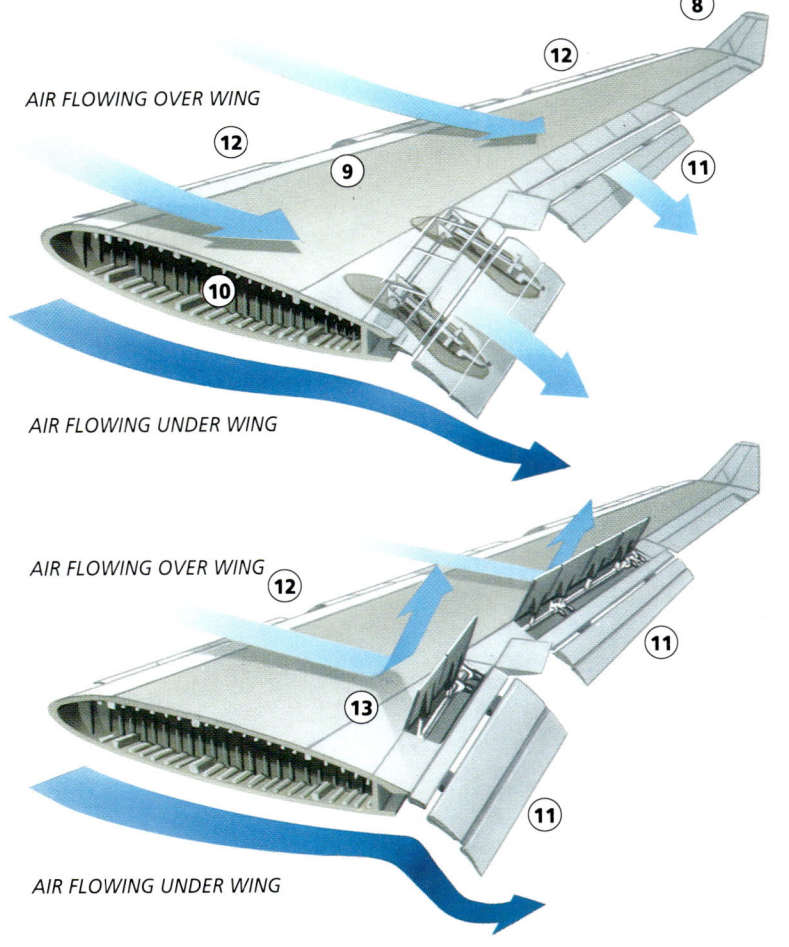

AIR FLOWING OVER WING

AIR FLOWING UNDER WING

AIR FLOWING OVER WING

AIR FLOWING UNDER WING

EXTENDING THE WING
Maximium lift is needed at take-off and landing, when speeds are slower. FLAPS fitted to the wing are used to extend the wing surface and exaggerate its curved profile in order to provide extra lift when needed. When a Jumbo takes off or lands, flaps extend outwards at the trailing (rear) edge of the wings. At take-off, they are set at a smaller angle than at landing. The 747's wing has a layered 'skirt' of three flaps with slots in between through which the air is channelled. Hinged flaps at the leading (front) edges of the wings also project forwards to extend the wing surface still further.

COMING TO A HALT
SPOILERS are used to help bring a 747 to a halt after it has landed. When the plane touches down, these flat surfaces mounted on the upper side of the wings flip upwards, immediately adding to the drag force (the resistance of the air to the plane moving through it). Suddenly, the air pressure is higher above the wing than below it, putting the full weight of the plane on its wheels. Spoilers can also be used like AILERONS when the pilot wishes to bank the plane (perform a rolling turn).

KEY
4 TAIL FIN
5 TAILPLANE
6 REAR PRESSURE BULKHEAD
7 LAVATORY
8 WINGLET
9 WING
10 INTERNAL STRUCTURE OF WING
11 FLAPS
12 FLAPS AT LEADING EDGE
13 SPOILERS
14 CREW REST AREA
15 ECONOMY-CLASS SEATING
16 WASTE TANKS
17 INSULATION (inside fuselage)
18 REAR BAGGAGE HOLD
19 LEADING EDGE FLAP MECHANISM
20 AIR SUPPLY DUCT
21 MAIN FUEL TANKS
22 AILERONS
23 ELEVATORS

▼ TUPOLEV Tu-95 (1952)
Since the Second World War, bombers were built to fly farther and farther. One, the American B-52, made the first non-stop flight around the world. The Soviets once competed with the Americans to build weapons that were just as effective as theirs. The Tu-95 long-range bomber aircraft was like a Soviet B-52. Fast (the fastest-ever propeller-driven aircraft), high-flying and as long as the width of a football pitch, the 'Bear' was also used to fly over the world's oceans and send back information on the enemy's naval positions. The pipe in its nose was used to take in fuel in mid-air from tanker aircraft.

BAC/AÉROSPATIALE CONCORDE (1969)
High-speed technology linked up with long-distance passenger air travel to make Concorde. It was not the first SUPERSONIC airliner to fly (the Soviet Tupolev-144, a very similar-looking aircraft, first took off in 1968), but it is the only type still in service. It incorporates a DELTA WING design (with no tailplane) and distinctive 'droop snoot', a needle-shaped nose which pivots downwards on landing to enable the pilots to see the runway. Flying at more than 18,000 metres, and at twice the speed of sound, Concorde has travelled from New York to London in less than 3 hours, half the time taken by other airliners. (right)

▲ NORTH AMERICAN X-15 (1959)
Like the XS-1, the X-15 was a rocket-powered aircraft, incapable of taking off by itself, and designed purely for speed. It did not disappoint: it is still today

▼ MIL Mi-6 (1957)
Fitting GAS TURBINE engines to a helicopter allowed designers to produce bigger and faster machines. About the same length and weight as some airliners of its time, the Soviet Mi-6 was for many years the largest helicopter in the world. It can seat 70 people, and is fitted with small wings which gives it extra lift for cruising. Its many roles include troop carrier, firefighter and component carrier for the oil industry. One version of it has extended wheel struts, enabling it to carry trucks or even small houses beneath it like a giant bird of prey.

▶ The Akron was steered by the crew inside the control car. There was also an emergency control position inside the leading edge of the airship's lower fin.

For my most beautiful bird.
JR

Beautiful Birds © Flying Eye Books, 2015.

This is a third edition.
First published in 2015 by Flying Eye Books, an imprint
of Nobrow Ltd. 27 Westgate Street, London, E8 3RL.

Text © Jean Roussen, 2015. Illustrations © Emmanuelle Walker, 2015.
Jean Roussen and Emmanuelle Walker have asserted their right under the Copyright,
Designs and Patents Act, 1988, to be identified as the author and illustrator of this Work.

All rights reserved. No part of this publication may be reproduced or transmitted in any
form or by any means, electronic or mechanical, including photocopying, recording or by any
information and storage retrieval system, without prior written consent from the publisher.

Published in the US by Nobrow (US) Inc.
Printed in Latvia on FSC® certified paper
ISBN: 978-1-909263-29-1

Order from www.flyingeyebooks.com

JEAN ROUSSEN
EMMANUELLE WALKER

BEAUTIFUL BIRDS

FLYING EYE BOOKS
LONDON | NEW YORK

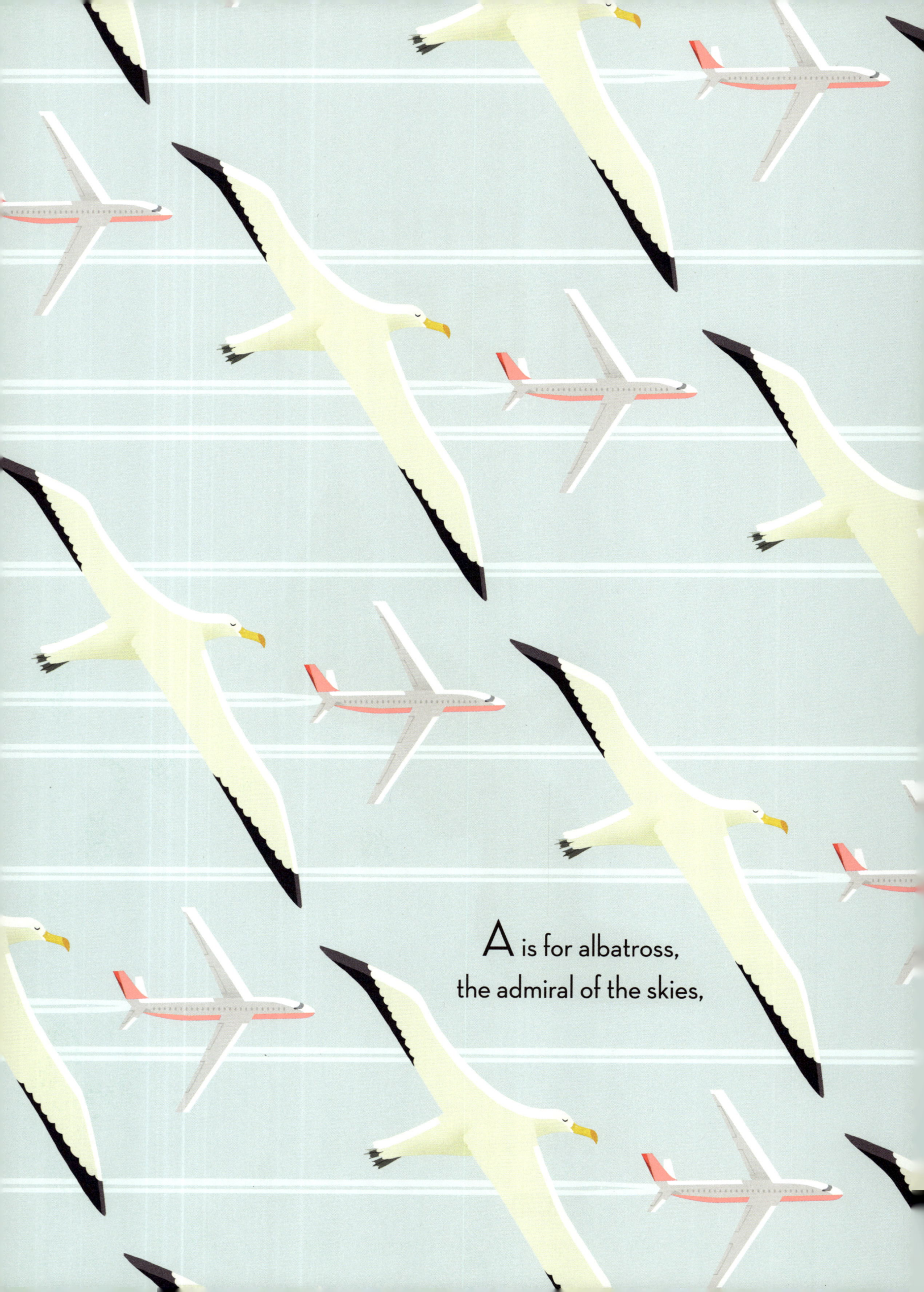

A is for albatross, the admiral of the skies,

B is for bee-eaters, BEWARE any bug that flies.

C is for cranes, both whooping and crowned,

C is for cockatoos, crests abound.

D is for dove, and the promise of peace and love,

E is for egret: its yellow eyes that pierce

and E is for eagle, majestic but fierce.

F is for finches of every shape and every size

and F is for flamingos with their long, graceful strides.

G is for geese in snow or on a farm,

don't get too close or one might bite your arm!

at 50 beats a second they're fast lil' things.

I is for ibis, jewels of the river Nile,

J is for jacana, perched on a crocodile.

K is for kakapo,
the parrot of the night

and K is for kiwi: two strange birds that lack flight.

L is for larks who sing songs so magnificent,

ON THE AIR

and mandarin ducks, the oddest of couples.

N is for nightingales
who sing us to sleep,

and for nuthatches who bore into trees deep.

O is for owls of all kinds with their ogling orbs,

it's also for orioles and
their greedy fruit hoards.

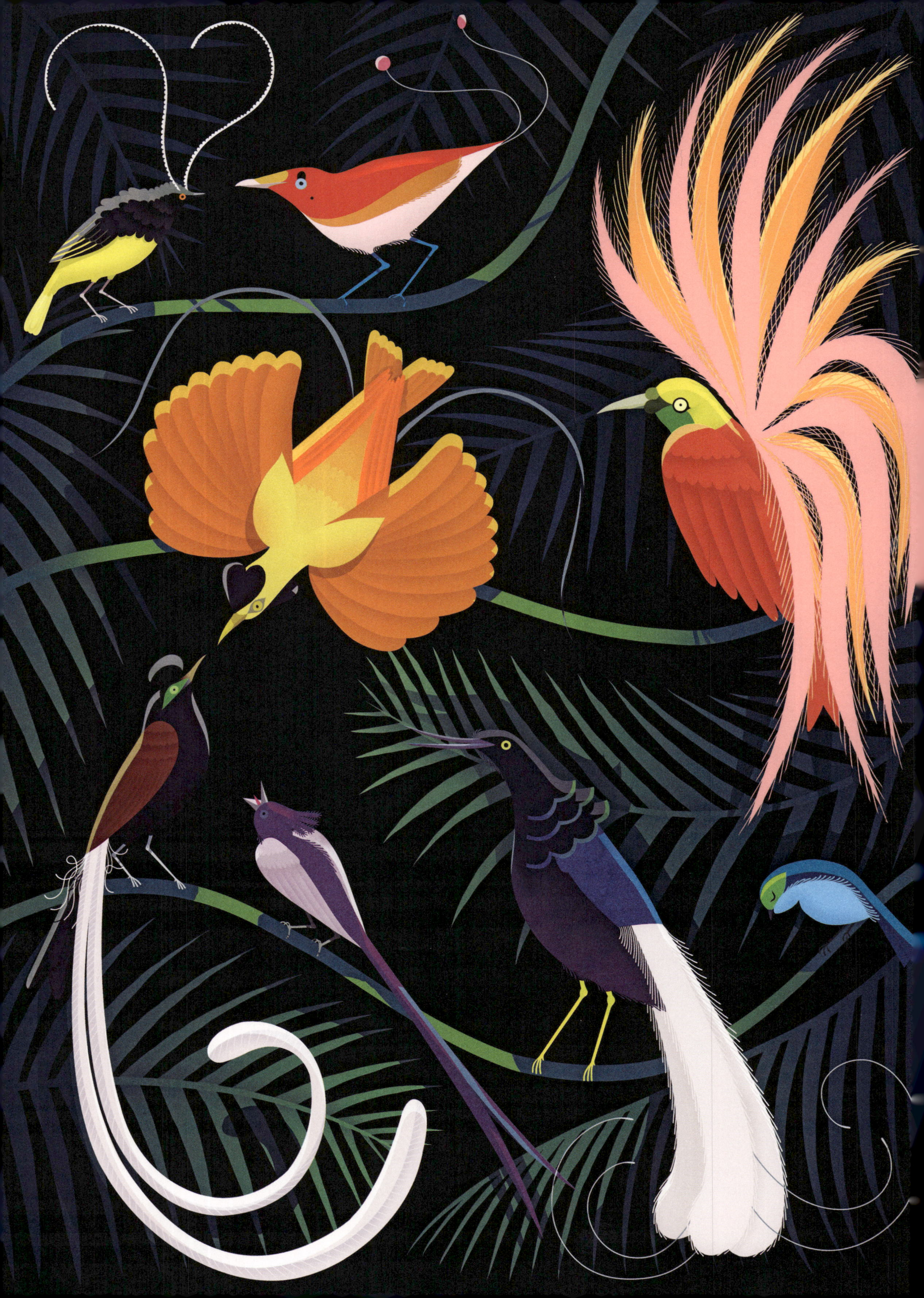

P is for paradise
and all of its birds,

P is for peacock,
it's the proudest,
I've heard...

Q is for the quetzal, a god among us,

Q is for quails with top-knots: what a big fuss!

R is for robin the sweetest of sweet, dashing and diving through snowfall and sleet.

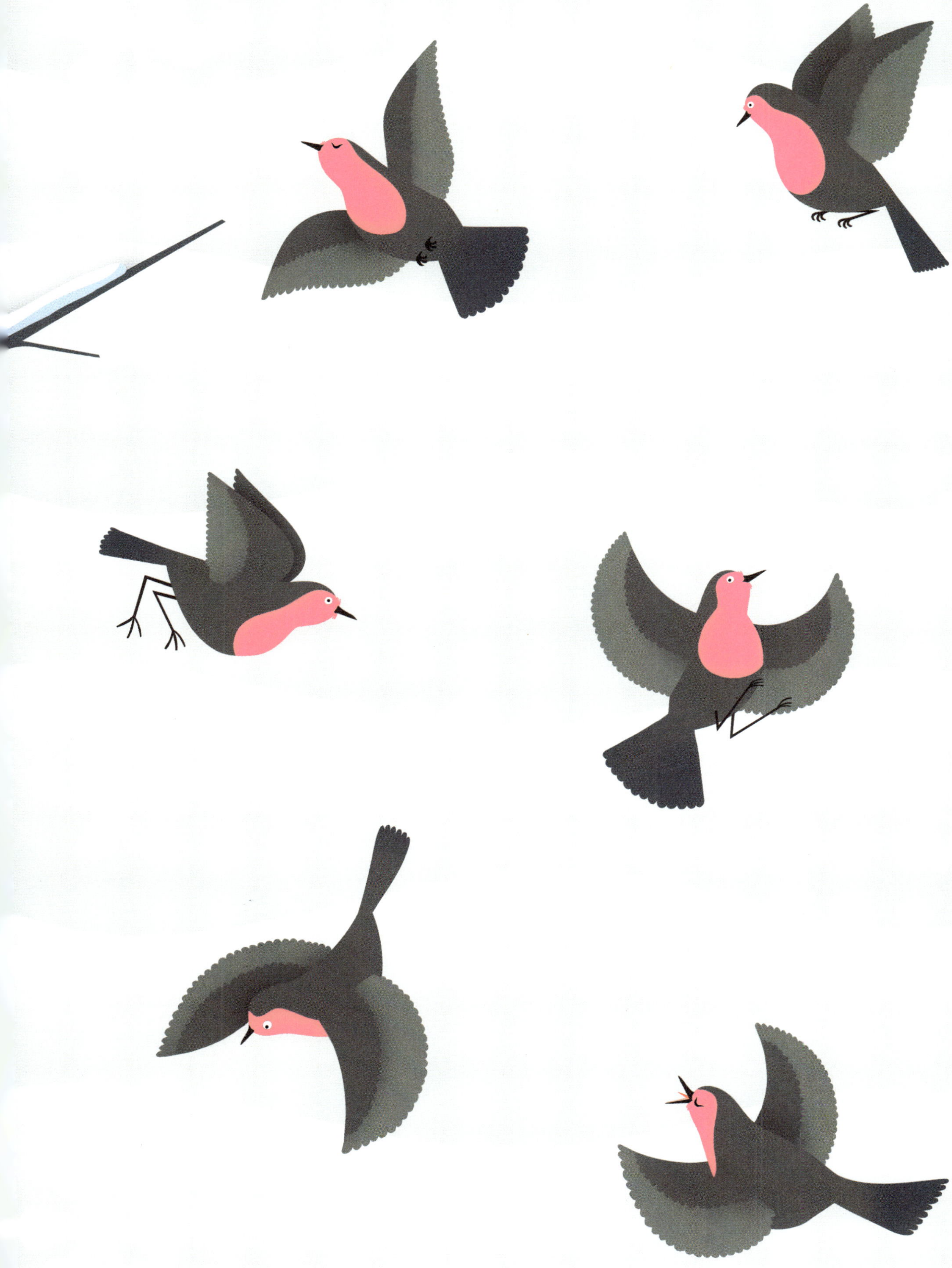

S is for swallow, acrobat of the air,

it's also for swan, who's the fairest of fair…?

T is for toucans and their tremendous hooked bills,

T is for tanagers with their polychrome quills.

U is for ultramarine: kingfisher, flycatcher and lorikeet,
It's a colour that in nature is really, truly, quite unique.

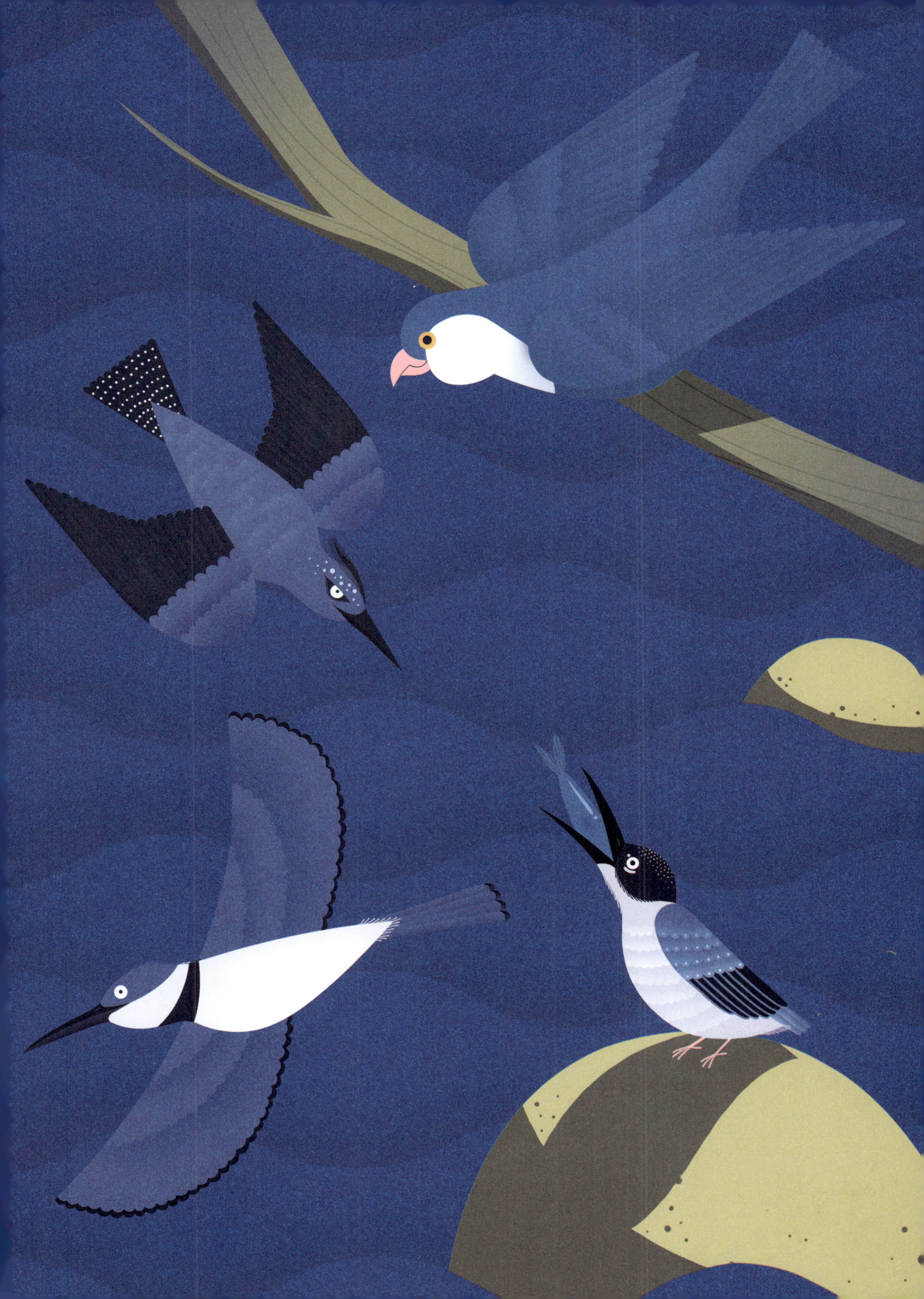

V is for a formation that's a rare sight to see,

W is for woodpeckers rapping away at a tree.

X is for xanthocephalus,
that means 'gold-head' in Greek,

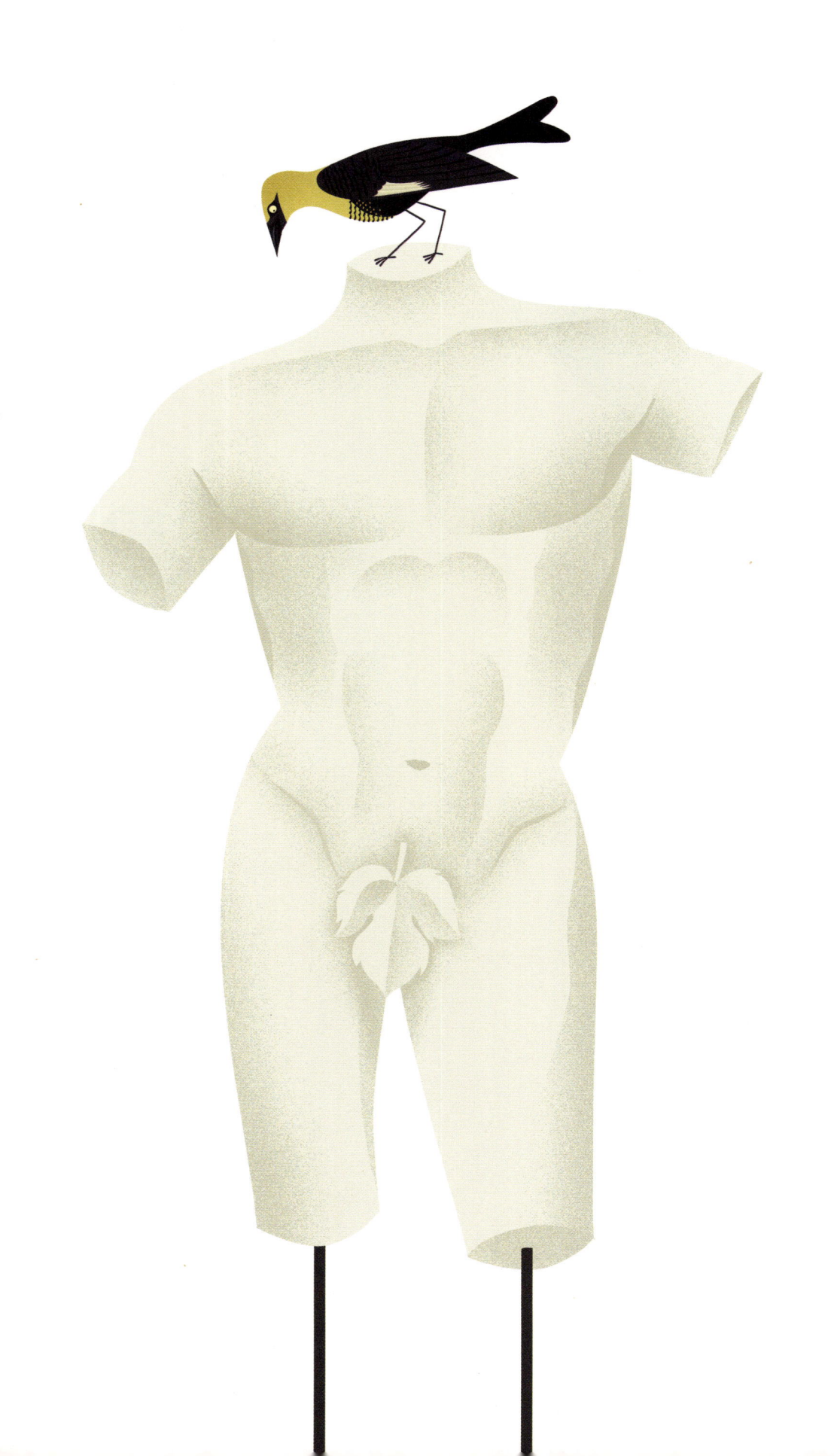

Y is for yorkshire canary:
yellow, from tail to beak.

Z is for zos-ter-o-pi-dae,
finding that bird just made my day.

Of all the birds in the skies and the trees,
There is only one that is the 'bee's knees',
Hmm... which of us could it possibly be?

The most beautiful bird,
of course, is me!